■ SCHOLASTIC

Pocket-Folder Center
Math

12 Ready-to-Go Centers That Motivate Children to Practice and Strengthen Essential Math Skills—Independently!

by Ada Goren

New York • Toronto • London • Auckland • Sydney
Mexico City • New Delhi • Hong Kong • Buenos Aires

Teaching *Resources*

To Dave, AJ, and Max—my three boys!

Edited by Immacula A. Rhodes
Cover design by Brian LaRossa
Interior design by Solas
Cover and interior illustrations by Rusty Fletcher

978-0-545-13037-0

2 3 4 5 6 7 8 9 10   17 16 15 14 13 12 11 10

Table of Contents

Pocket-Folder Centers

Looking for ways to get children working independently on essential skills? If so, you'll appreciate the opportunities offered by *Pocket-Folder Centers in Color: Math: Grades K–1*, a collection of learning centers that targets math skills every child needs to master.

Research shows that understanding math concepts is fundamental to developing proficiency and becoming an autonomous learner. The center activities in this book provide children of all learning styles with a motivating, fun way to practice and build skills independently while helping them meet important math standards. (See "What the Research Says" and "Meeting the Math Standards," page 9, for more.) After they do each activity, children complete a practice page that gives them additional reinforcement in the targeted skill. Answer keys are also included, making the centers self-correcting and allowing children to assess their work independently.

Everything you need is here and ready to assemble—saving you countless hours of preparation time. The pocket-folder centers are a snap to set up and store: Just glue the labels to the folders, pop the full-color activity mats and copies of the practice pages into the pockets, and you've got twelve instant learning center activities. Children will have fun learning as they match shapes in The Shape Gallery, compare number sets in What's the Buzz?, practice addition facts in Race to the Moon!, complete and analyze a graph in Gems of the Sea, count money in Duck's Diner, measure with nonstandard units in Monkey Measures, and much more.

What's Inside

All the materials needed for the pocket-folder centers are included in this resource. In addition, a reproducible class record sheet that helps you chart children's use of the activities and a full-color label to use on the storage container for the centers are included.

Each center activity includes the following:

❧ an introductory page for the teacher that shows how the center is assembled

❧ a list of materials needed to prepare and use the activity

❧ step-by-step assembly directions

❧ a front label with directions that explain to children how to use the activity

❧ labels for the practice pages and activity mat to attach to the folder pockets

❧ an answer key

❧ a full-color activity mat

❧ activity cards

❧ a reproducible practice page to provide additional reinforcement

❧ some activities also include additional manipulatives, such as a game cube and game markers

practice pages

answer key

pocket labels

front label

activity mat

cards

counters

Making the Pocket-Folder Centers

In addition to the center activity pages,
you will need the following:

- 12 colorful, two-pocket folders
  (without prongs)
- scissors
- glue stick or rubber cement
- craft knife
- zipper plastic bags

TIPS

- Glue the pocket-folder labels and
  answer key to each folder. Then
  laminate the folder, activity mat,
  cards, and markers for durability.

- After laminating the folder, use a craft
  knife to slit and re-open the pockets.

- For extra durability, back the activity
  mats and cards with tagboard,
  then laminate.

- Before cutting the activity cards
  apart, make additional color or
  black-and-white copies to have
  on hand in case pieces are lost.

Storage Ideas

Laminate the full-color label (page 11) and
attach it to your pocket-folder storage container.
Keep the pocket-folder centers in any of these places:

- learning center
- vertical file tray
- file box
- file cabinet
- bookshelf
- plastic stacking crate
- large storage tub

Pocket-Folder
Centers:
Math

Using the Pocket-Folder Centers

Here are some suggestions for using the pocket-folder centers with children:

- Before introducing the pocket-folder activities to children, conduct mini-lessons to review the math concepts used in each center.

- Demonstrate for children how to use the pocket-folder activities. (See sidebar at right.)

- Store the pocket folders in a learning center and encourage children to use them for an independent learning activity before or after school, during free-choice time, when they have finished other tasks, or while you work with other individuals or small groups.

- When children complete a center, have them place their practice page in a specified location. You can use the practice pages to track progress and assess skills.

- Keep the centers handy for use as quick assessments or for volunteer tutors to use as instructional tools.

- Send the pocket-folder centers home with children to give them extra practice and to encourage family involvement in their learning.

Using the Centers Is Easy!

1. Open the folder, take out the activity mat, accessories, and a practice page. Close the folder.

2. Use the mat and cards to complete the activity.

3. Open the folder and check your work on the answer key.

4. Close the folder and complete the practice page.

5. Open the folder again and use the answer key to check your work.

Getting the Most Out of Pocket-Folder Centers

Here are a few more ways to get the most use and benefit from the centers:

CLASSROOM MANAGEMENT: Write children's names on a copy of the Class Record Sheet (page 10) and post it near your pocket-folder centers storage container. Then, whenever children complete their assigned centers, they can check it off on the chart. They can also check the chart to see which centers they still need to complete.

DIFFERENTIATION: Fill in children's names on the Class Record Sheet. Cross out the centers that individual children do not need to complete—either because they are not ready for the skill or they have already shown competence in it. Post the chart and have children mark the box for each assigned center that they complete.

ASSESSMENT: Both the centers and the practice pages can be used as quick and engaging informal assessments. Simply observe children at work at a center. Ask them to think aloud as they make decisions about their responses. Or check their work when they have completed the center and practice page to determine their level of success with the skill. You might use the results when conferencing with children about their progress. If desired, use the Class Record Sheet (page 10) to keep track of children's progress by simply recording a plus (+) or minus (−) to indicate whether they have mastered the skill or need additional instruction or reinforcement.

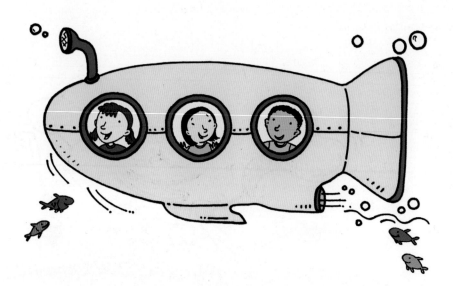

What the Research Says

To become proficient in math, children must be able to understand and meaningfully apply their factual and conceptual knowledge in different settings and situations. According to NCTM, in its *Principles and Standards for School Mathematics* (2000), "A major goal of school mathematics programs is to create autonomous learners, and learning with understanding supports this goal. Students learn more and learn better when they can take control of their learning by defining their goals and monitoring their own progress. When challenged with appropriately chosen tasks, students become confident in their ability to tackle the difficult problems, eager to figure things out on their own, flexible in exploring mathematical ideas and trying alternative solution paths, and willing to persevere."

Meeting the Math Standards

Connections to the McREL Math Standards

Mid-continent Research for Education and Learning (McREL), a nationally recognized nonprofit organization, has compiled and evaluated national and state standards—and proposed what teachers should provide for their K–1 students to grow proficient in math. The activities in this book support the following standards:

Understands and applies basic and advanced properties of the concepts of numbers including:
- Understands that numbers represent quantities
- Counts to ten or higher
- Counts whole numbers (cardinal and ordinal numbers)
- Knows the written numerals 0–9
- Understands the concept of position in a sequence
- Understands basic whole number relationships

Uses basic and advanced procedures while performing the processes of computation including:
- Adds and subtracts whole numbers

Understands and applies basic and advanced properties of the concepts of measurement including:
- Knows processes for telling time, counting money, and measuring length, using basic standard units

Understands and applies basic and advanced properties of the concepts of geometry including:
- Sorts and groups objects by attributes
- Understands basic properties of and similarities and differences between simple geometric shapes

Understands and applies basic and advanced concepts of statistics and data analysis including:
- Knows that graphs represent information
- Collects and represents information in simple graphs

Understands and applies basic and advanced properties of functions and algebra
- Understands, repeats, and extends simple patterns
- Recognizes a wide variety of patterns

Source: Kendall, J. S., & Marzano, R. J. (2004). *Content knowledge: A Compendium of Standards and Benchmarks for K-12 Education.* Aurora, CO: Mid-continent Research for Education and Learning. Online database: http://www.mcrel.org/standards-benchmarks/

Connections to the NCTM Math Standards

The activities in this book are also designed to support you in meeting the following K–1 standards—including process standards, such as problem solving, reasoning and proof, and communication—recommended by the National Council of Teachers of Mathematics (NCTM):

Numbers and Operations
Understand numbers, ways of representing numbers, relationships among numbers, and number systems
- Count with understanding and recognize "how many" in sets of objects
- Develop understanding of the relative position and magnitude of whole numbers and of ordinal and cardinal numbers and their connections
- Connect number words and numerals to the quantities they represent

Understand meanings of operations and how they relate to one another
- Develop fluency with basic number combinations for addition and subtraction
- Use a variety of methods and tools to compute, including objects, mental computation, and paper and pencil

Algebra
Understand patterns, relations, and functions
- Recognize, describe, and extend patterns
- Analyze how repeating patterns are generated

Geometry
Analyze characteristics and properties of two- and three-dimensional geometric shapes
- Recognize, name, compare, and sort two- and three-dimensional shapes

Measurement
Understand measurable attributes of objects and the units, systems, and processes of measurement
- Recognize the attributes of length and time
- Understand how to measure using nonstandard and standard units

Apply appropriate techniques, tools, and formulas to determine measurement
- Measure with multiple copies of units of the same size, such as paper clips
- Use tools to measure

Data Analysis and Probability
Formulate questions that can be addressed with data and collect, organize, and display relevant data to answer them
- Sort and classify objects according to their attributes and organize data about the objects
- Represent data using concrete objects, pictures, and graphs

Source: National Council of Teachers of Mathematics. (2000). *Principles and Standards for School Mathematics.* Reston, VA: NCTM. www.nctm.org

Pocket-Folder Centers

CLASS RECORD SHEET

Student	The Shape Gallery	Colorful Crawlers	Bunny's Bubbles	What's the Buzz?	Elephants on Parade	Sam's Jams	Race to the Moon!	Submarine Scene	Gems of the Sea	Duck's Diner	Game Time!	Monkey Measures

Pocket-Folder Centers: Math

The Shape Gallery

How to Assemble

1. Cut out the front label on page 15. Glue it to the front of the pocket folder.

2. Cut out the pocket labels and answer key on page 17. Glue them to the inside of the folder, as shown.

3. Cut out the activity mat and picture cards on pages 19, 21, and 23. Store the cards in the zipper plastic bag.

4. Make multiple copies of the practice page on page 14.

5. Place the practice pages in the left pocket and the activity mat and cards in the right pocket.

MATERIALS

❖ pages 14–23

❖ two-pocket folder

❖ scissors

❖ glue

❖ zipper plastic bag

practice pages

answer key

The Shape Gallery
Practice Pages

The Shape Gallery
Activity Mat and Cards

pocket labels

front label

activity mat

cards

Name_____ Date_____

Frame It!

Look at the shape of each frame.
Find the pictures with the same shape.
Color them.

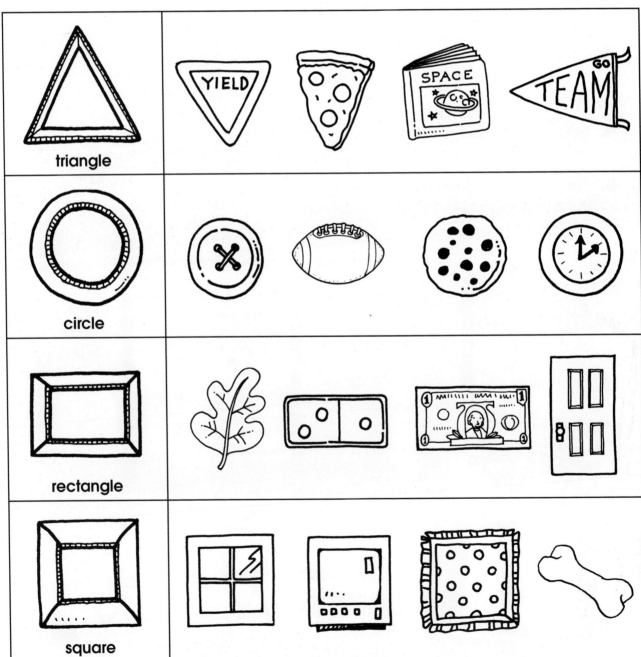

triangle

circle

rectangle

square

The Shape Gallery Practice Page • Pocket-Folder Centers: *Math* © 2010 by Ada Goren, Scholastic Teaching Resources

The Shape Gallery

SKILL Matching Shapes

What To Do:

1. Look at each picture card.
   What shape is the picture?

2. Look at the mat.
   Find the frame that has the same shape.
   Put the card on that frame.

3. Check your answers.

4. Complete a practice page.

5. Check your answers.

The Shape Gallery
Practice Pages

The Shape Gallery
Activity Mat and Cards

The Shape Gallery
Answers

Practice Page

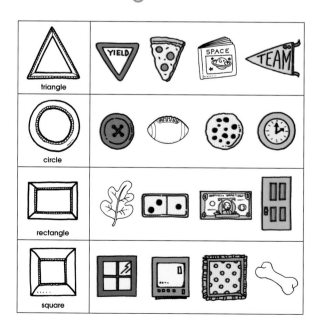

Activity Mat

rectangle: book, dollar bill, domino, door, juice box, ruler

circle: beach ball, button, clock, cookie, penny, ring

square: cracker, crayon box, mat, stamp, television, window

triangle: party hat, pennant, pizza, tent, watermelon, yield sign

The Shape Gallery

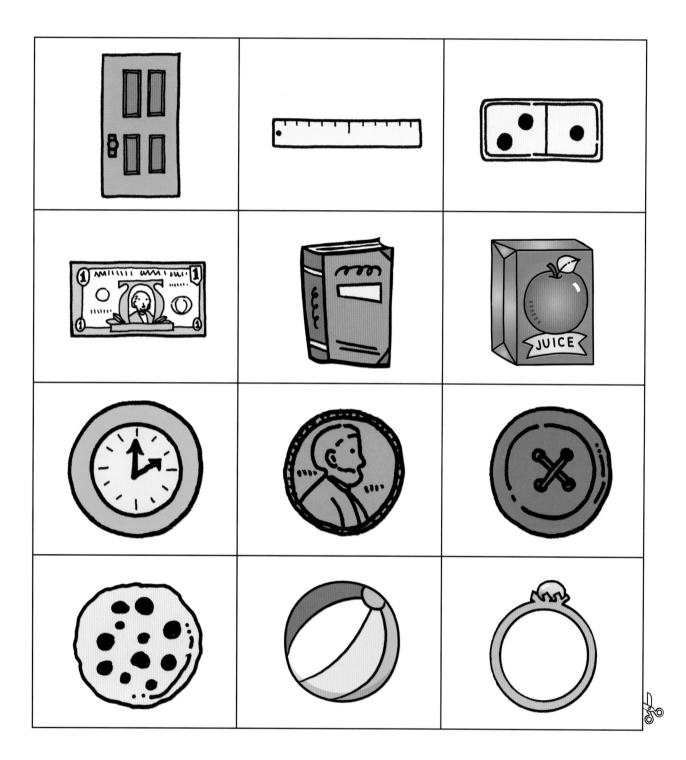

Colorful Crawlers

How to Assemble

1. Cut out the front label on page 27. Glue it to the front of the pocket folder.

2. Cut out the pocket labels and answer key on page 29. Glue them to the inside of the folder, as shown.

3. Cut out the activity mat and pattern cards on pages 31 and 33. Store the cards in the zipper plastic bag.

4. Make multiple copies of the practice page on page 26.

5. Place the practice pages in the left pocket and the activity mat and cards in the right pocket.

MATERIALS

❖ pages 26–33

❖ two-pocket folder

❖ scissors

❖ glue

❖ zipper plastic bag

TIP: Have scissors and glue handy for children to complete the practice page.

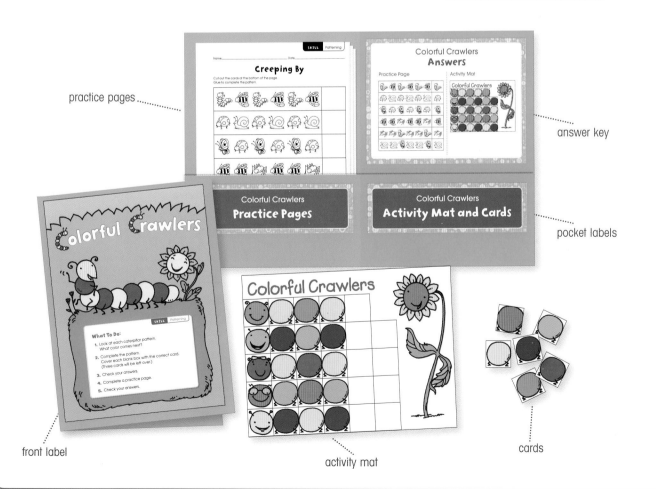

practice pages

answer key

pocket labels

front label

activity mat

cards

Name_____ Date_____

Creeping By

Cut out the cards at the bottom of the page.
Glue to complete the pattern.

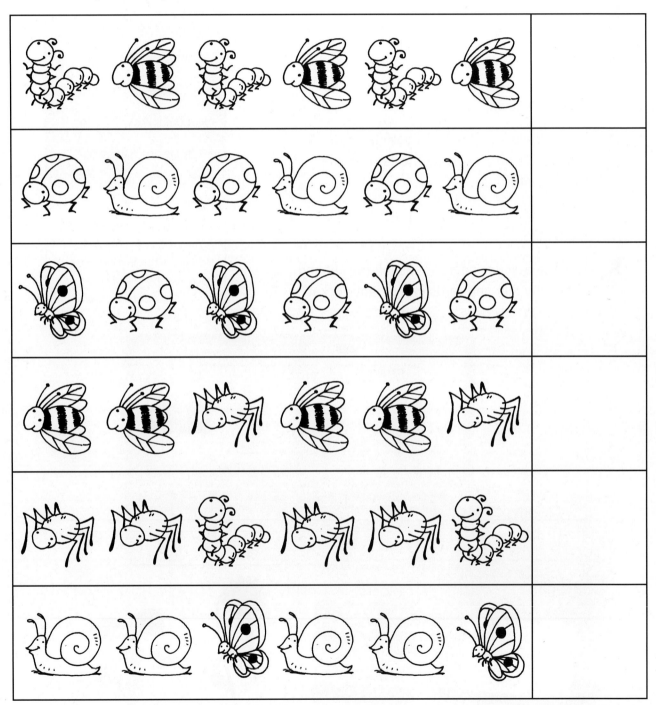

Colorful Crawlers

SKILL Patterning

What To Do:

1. Look at each caterpillar pattern.
   What color comes next?

2. Complete the pattern.
   Cover each blank box with the correct card.
   (Three cards will be left over.)

3. Check your answers.

4. Complete a practice page.

5. Check your answers.

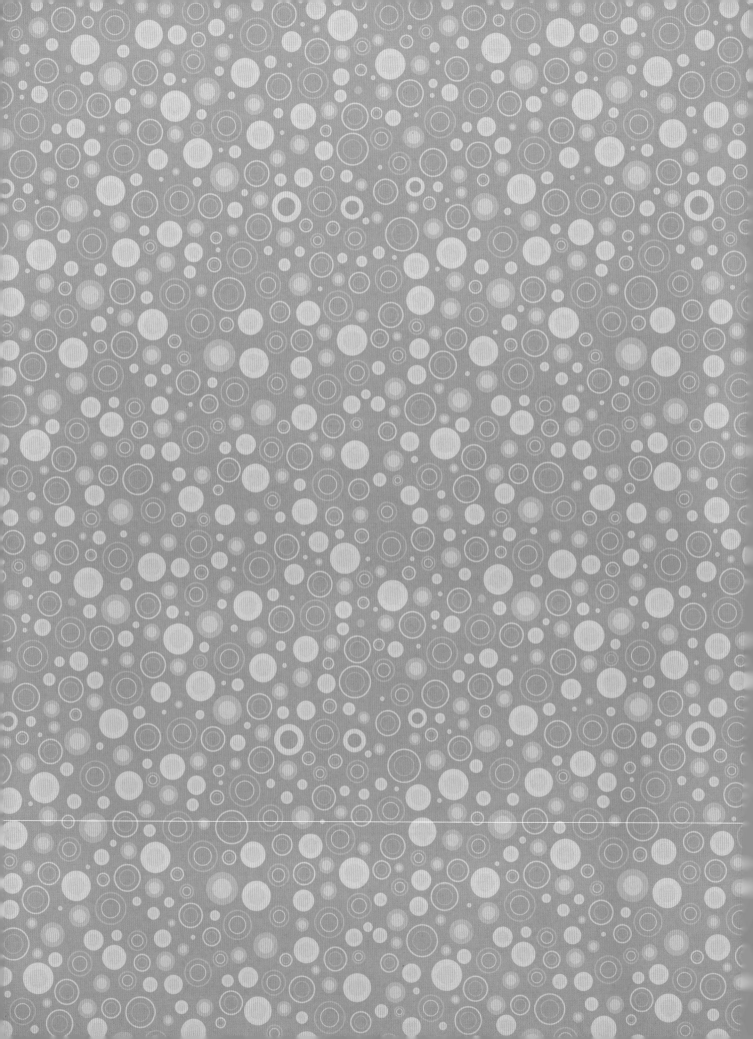

Colorful Crawlers
Practice Pages

Colorful Crawlers
Activity Mat and Cards

Colorful Crawlers
Answers

Practice Page

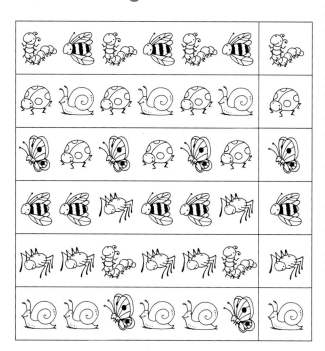

Activity Mat

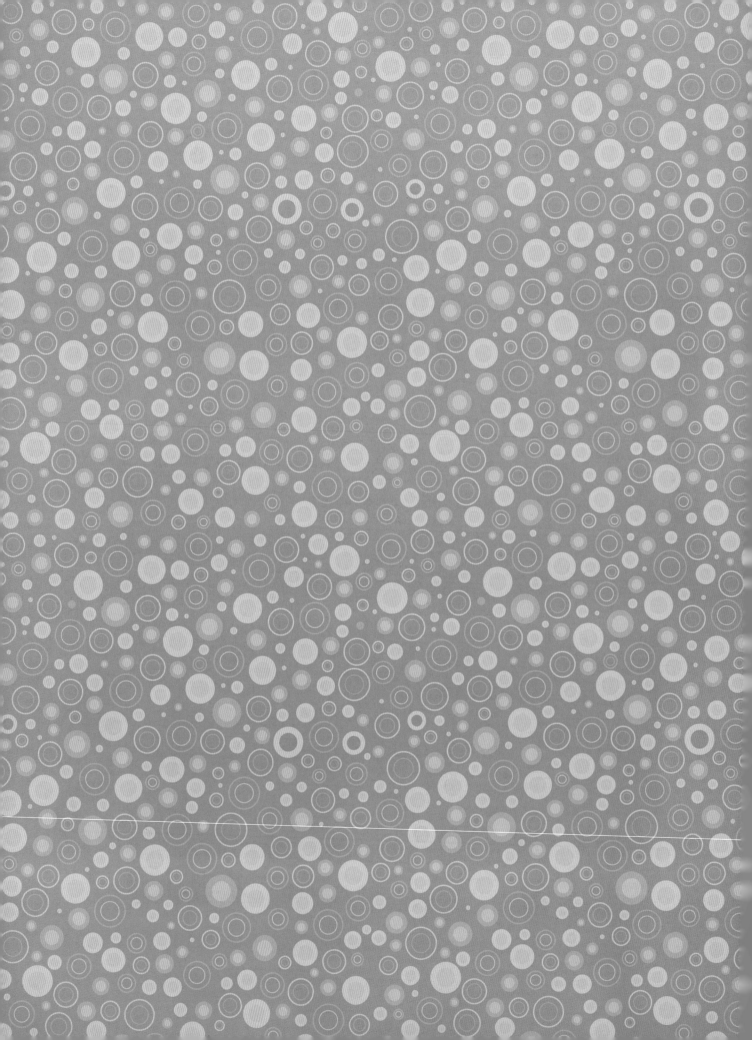

Colorful Crawlers

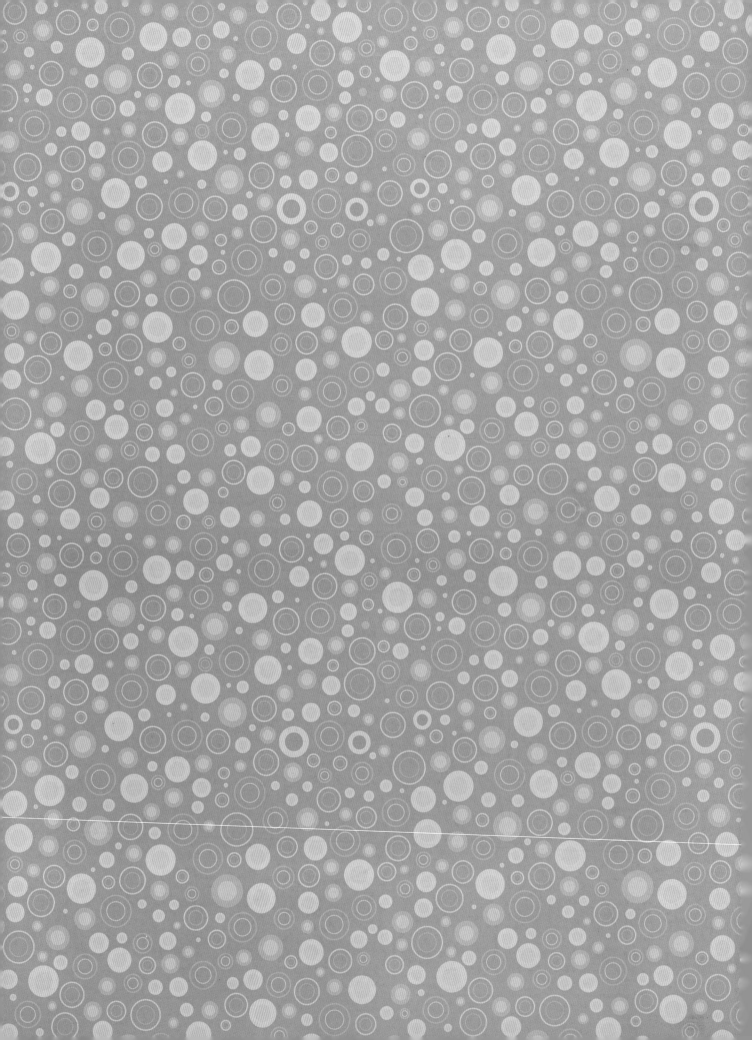

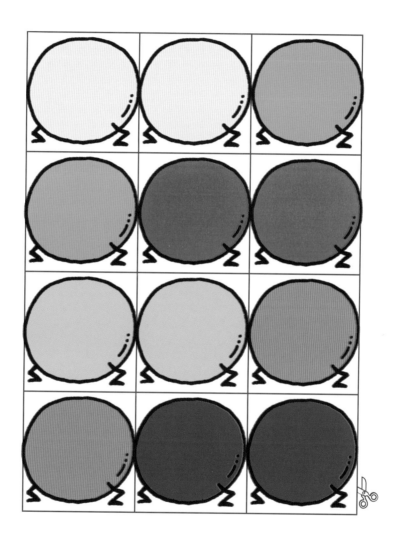

Bunny's Bubbles

How to Assemble

1. Cut out the front label on page 37. Glue it to the front of the pocket folder.

2. Cut out the pocket labels and answer key on page 39. Glue them to the inside of the folder, as shown.

3. Cut out the activity mat, number cards, and bubble counters on pages 41 and 43. Store the cards and counters in the zipper plastic bag.

4. Make multiple copies of the practice page on page 36.

5. Place the practice pages in the left pocket and the activity mat, cards, and counters in the right pocket.

MATERIALS

❖ pages 36–43

❖ two-pocket folder

❖ scissors

❖ glue

❖ zipper plastic bag

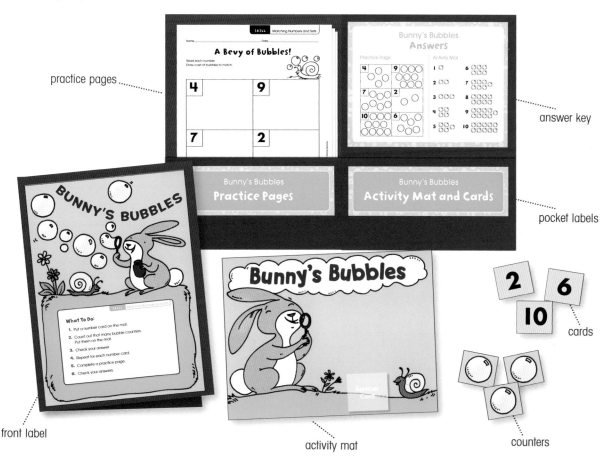

practice pages

answer key

pocket labels

front label

activity mat

cards

counters

Name_____ Date_____

A Bevy of Bubbles!

Read each number.
Draw a set of bubbles to match.

4	**9**
7	**2**
10	**6**

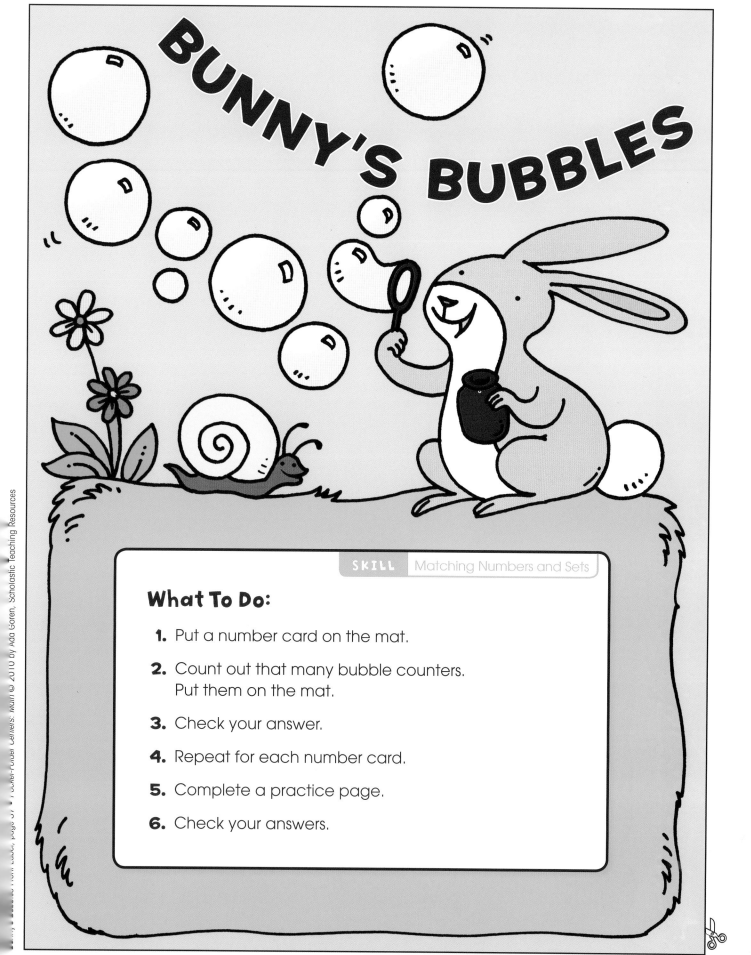

BUNNY'S BUBBLES

What To Do:

1. Put a number card on the mat.

2. Count out that many bubble counters. Put them on the mat.

3. Check your answer.

4. Repeat for each number card.

5. Complete a practice page.

6. Check your answers.

Bunny's Bubbles
Activity Mat and Cards

Bunny's Bubbles
Answers

Practice Page

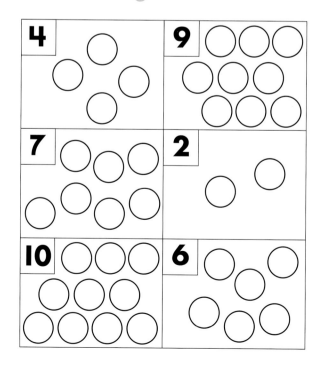

Activity Mat

1

2

3

4

5

6

7

8

9

10

1	2	3	4
5	6	7	8
9	10		

What's the Buzz?

How to Assemble

1. Cut out the front label on page 47. Glue it to the front of the pocket folder.

2. Cut out the pocket labels and answer key on page 49. Glue them to the inside of the folder, as shown.

3. Cut out the activity mat, number cards, and bee counters on pages 51, 53, and 55. Store the cards and counters in the zipper plastic bag.

4. Cut a 12-inch length of yarn. Put it in the plastic bag.

5. Make multiple copies of the practice page on page 46.

6. Place the practice pages in the left pocket and the activity mat, cards, counters, and yarn in the right pocket.

MATERIALS

❖ pages 46–55

❖ two-pocket folder

❖ scissors

❖ glue

❖ zipper plastic bag

❖ 12-inch length of yarn

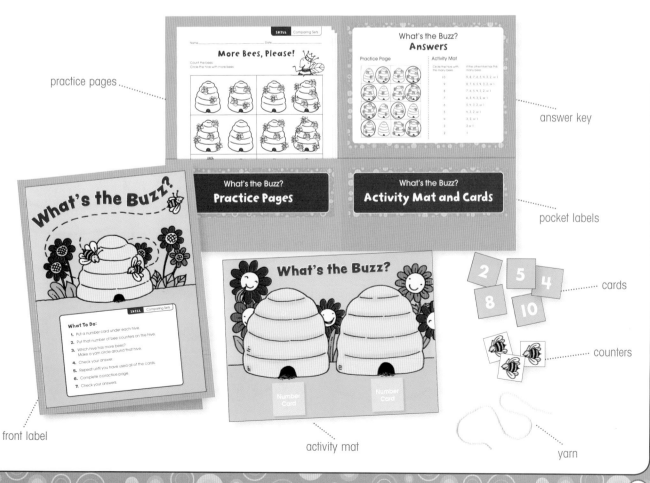

practice pages

answer key

pocket labels

cards

counters

front label

activity mat

yarn

Name_____ Date_____

More Bees, Please!

Count the bees.
Circle the hive with more bees.

What's the Buzz? Practice Page • Pocket-Folder Centers: Math © 2010 by Ada Goren, Scholastic Teaching Resources

What's the Buzz?

SKILL Comparing Sets

What To Do:

1. Put a number card under each hive.

2. Put that number of bee counters on the hive.

3. Which hive has more bees?
   Make a yarn circle around that hive.

4. Check your answer.

5. Repeat until you have used all of the cards.

6. Complete a practice page.

7. Check your answers.

What's the Buzz?
Practice Pages

What's the Buzz?
Activity Mat and Cards

What's the Buzz?
Answers

Practice Page

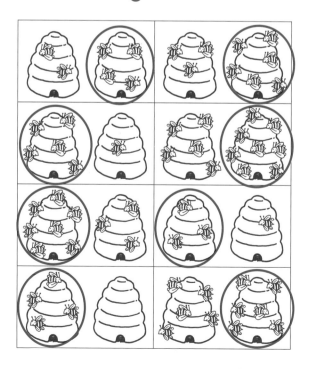

Activity Mat

Circle the hive with this many bees:	If the other hive has this many bees:
10	9, 8, 7, 6, 5, 4, 3, 2, or 1
9	8, 7, 6, 5, 4, 3, 2, or 1
8	7, 6, 5, 4, 3, 2, or 1
7	6, 5, 4, 3, 2, or 1
6	5, 4, 3, 2, or 1
5	4, 3, 2, or 1
4	3, 2, or 1
3	2 or 1
2	1

What's the Buzz?

Number Card

Number Card

1	2	3
4	5	6
7	8	9

10

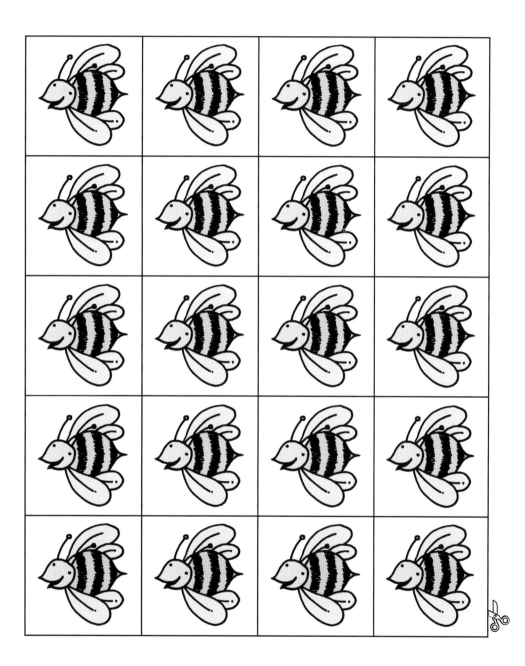

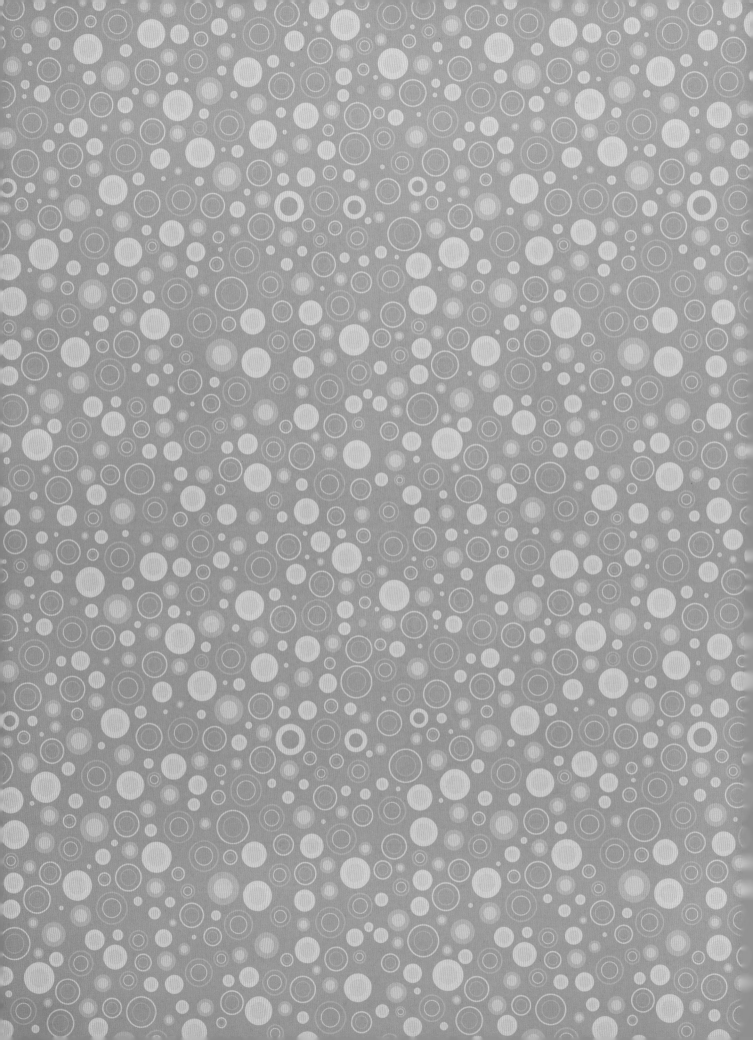

Elephants on Parade

How to Assemble

1. Cut out the front label on page 59. Glue it to the front of the pocket folder.

2. Cut out the pocket labels and answer key on page 61. Glue them to the inside of the folder, as shown.

3. Cut out the activity mat and number cards on pages 63 and 65. Store the cards in the zipper plastic bag.

4. Make multiple copies of the practice page on page 58.

5. Place the practice pages in the left pocket and the activity mat and cards in the right pocket.

MATERIALS

❖ pages 58–65

❖ two-pocket folder

❖ scissors

❖ glue

❖ zipper plastic bag

TIP: Have scissors and glue handy for children to complete the practice page.

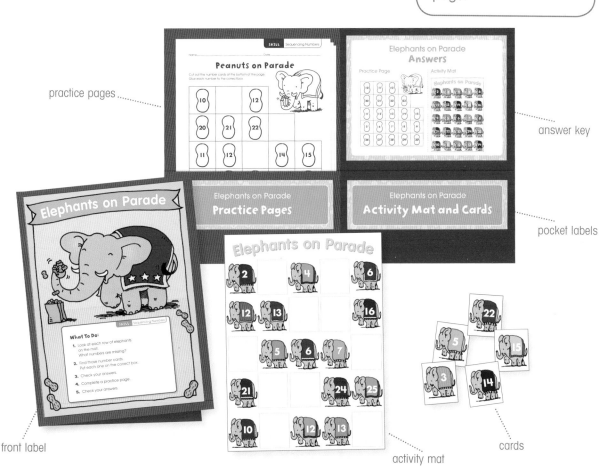

practice pages

answer key

pocket labels

front label

activity mat

cards

Name_____ Date_____

Peanuts on Parade

Cut out the number cards at the bottom of the page.
Glue each number to the correct box.

10		12
20	21	22
11	12		14	15
	6	7		9
26	27	28	29	

  13  5   30   23   11  8

Elephants on Parade

SKILL Sequencing Numbers

What To Do:

1. Look at each row of elephants on the mat.
   What numbers are missing?

2. Find those number cards.
   Put each one on the correct box.

3. Check your answers.

4. Complete a practice page.

5. Check your answers.

Elephants on Parade
Practice Pages

Elephants on Parade
Activity Mat and Cards

Elephants on Parade
Answers

Practice Page

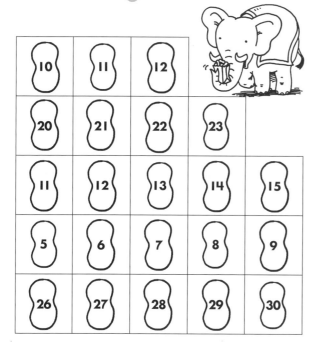

Activity Mat

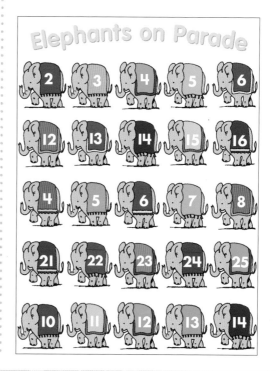

Elephants on Parade

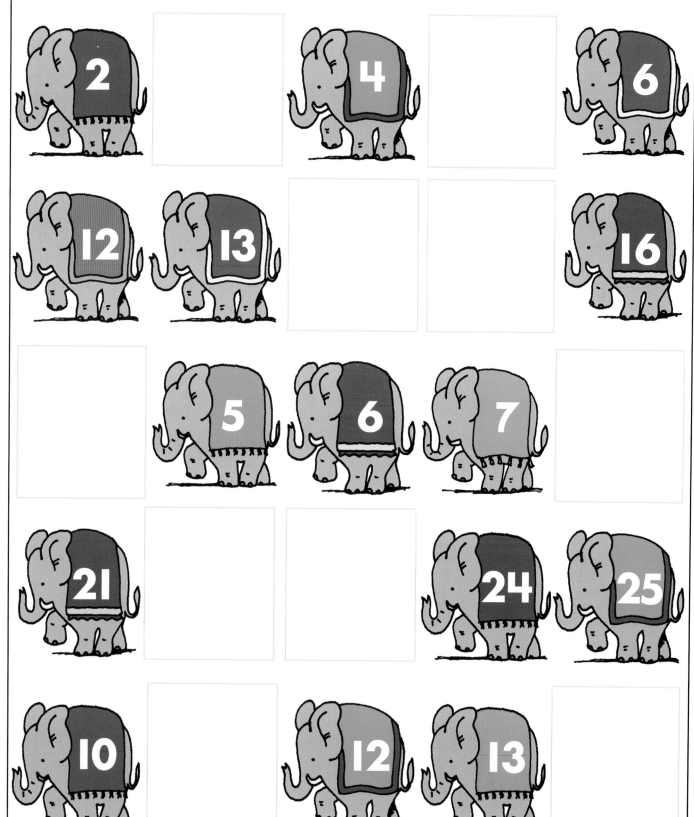

Sam's Jams

How to Assemble

1. Cut out the front label on page 69.
Glue it to the front of the pocket folder.

2. Cut out the pocket labels and answer key
on page 71. Glue them to the inside of the
folder, as shown.

3. Cut out the activity mat and number cards
on pages 73 and 75. Store one set of the cards
in the zipper plastic bag.

4. Make multiple copies of the practice page
on page 68.

5. Place the practice pages in the left pocket and
the activity mat and cards in the right pocket.

MATERIALS

❖ pages 68–75

❖ two-pocket folder

❖ scissors

❖ glue

❖ zipper plastic bag

TIP: Use the extra set of
number cards (page 75) to
replace worn or lost cards.

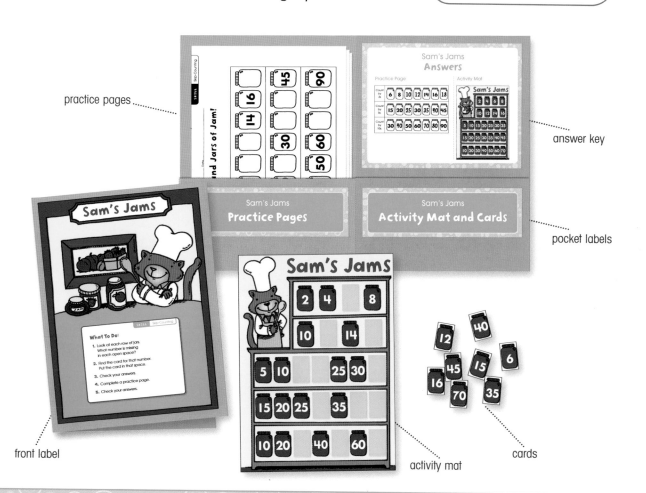

practice pages

answer key

pocket labels

front label

activity mat

cards

Name _____

Date _____

Jars and Jars of Jam!

Skip-count the jars.
Write the missing numbers.

Count by 2s.	6	8			14	16	
Count by 5s.	15	20		30			45
Count by 10s.	30		50	60			90

Sam's Jams

What To Do:

1. Look at each row of jars. What number is missing in each open space?

2. Find the card for that number. Put the card in that space.

3. Check your answers.

4. Complete a practice page.

5. Check your answers.

Sam's Jams
Practice Pages

Sam's Jams
Activity Mat and Cards

Sam's Jams
Answers

Practice Page

Count by 2s	6	8	10	12	14	16	18
Count by 5s.	15	20	25	30	35	40	45
Count by 10s.	30	40	50	60	70	80	90

Activity Mat

Sam's Jams

2	4	6	8
10	12	14	16

5	10	15	20	25	30	35
15	20	25	30	35	40	45
10	20	30	40	50	60	70

Sam's Jams

| 2 | 4 | | 8 |
| 10 | | 14 | |

5	10			25	30	
15	20	25		35		
10	20		40		60	

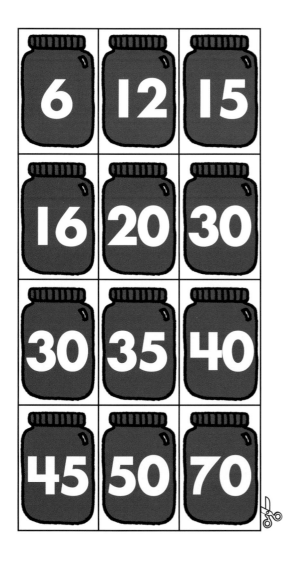

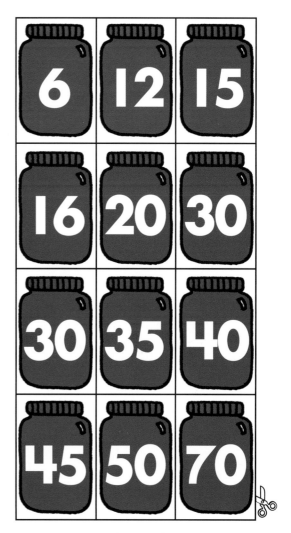

extra cards

Race to the Moon!

How to Assemble

1. Cut out the front label on page 79. Glue it to the front of the pocket folder.

2. Cut out the pocket labels and answer key on page 81. Glue them to the inside of the folder, as shown.

3. Cut out the activity mat, star counters, and game markers on pages 83, 85, and 87. Store the counters and markers in a zipper plastic bag.

4. Cut out and assemble the game cube on page 87.

5. Make multiple copies of the practice page on page 78.

6. Place the practice pages in the left pocket and the activity mat, counters, and markers in the right pocket.

MATERIALS

❖ pages 78–87

❖ two-pocket folder

❖ scissors

❖ glue

❖ zipper plastic bag

TIP: Place the game cube in a zipper plastic bag. Label the bag and keep it in a basket near the game.

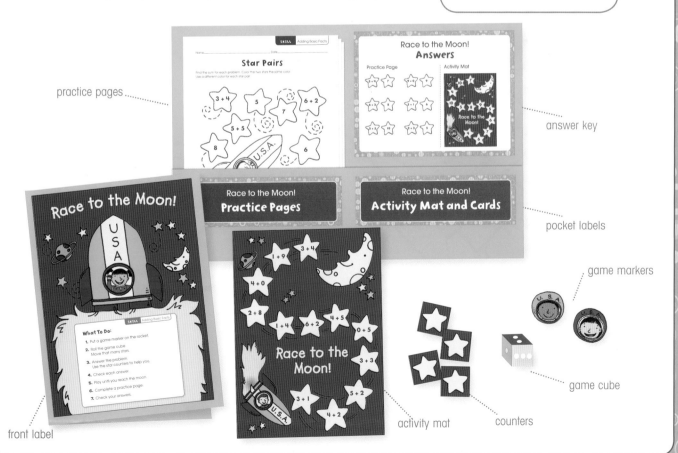

practice pages

answer key

pocket labels

game markers

game cube

activity mat

counters

front label

Name_____ Date_____

Star Pairs

Find the sum for each problem. Color the two stars the same color.
Use a different color for each star pair.

Race to the Moon!

What To Do:

1. Put a game marker on the rocket.

2. Roll the game cube.
   Move that many stars.

3. Answer the problem.
   Use the star counters to help you.

4. Check each answer.

5. Play until you reach the moon.

6. Complete a practice page.

7. Check your answers.

Race to the Moon!
Practice Pages

Race to the Moon!
Activity Mat and Cards

Race to the Moon!
Answers

Practice Page

3 + 4   7   9 + 0   9

6 + 2   8   5 + 1   6

5 + 5   10   2 + 3   5

Activity Mat

Race to the Moon!

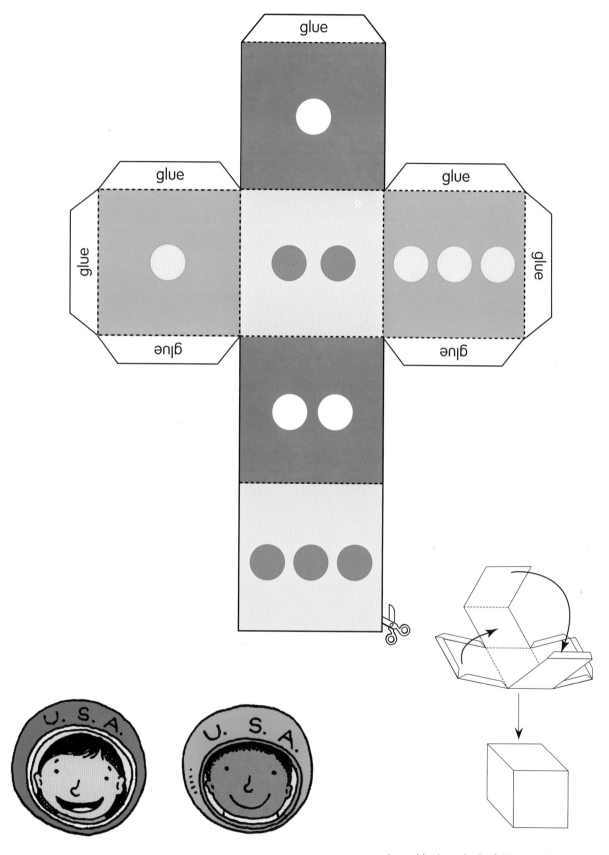

glue

glue

glue

glue

glue

glue

U. S. A.

U. S. A.

Assemble the cube by folding as shown. Glue closed.

Submarine Scene

How to Assemble

1. Cut out the front label on page 91.
Glue it to the front of the pocket folder.

2. Cut out the pocket labels and answer key
on page 93. Glue them to the inside of the
folder, as shown.

3. Cut out the activity mat, number cards, and seashell
counters on pages 95, 97 and 99. Store the cards
and counters in the zipper plastic bag.

4. Make multiple copies of the practice page
on page 90.

5. Place the practice pages in the left pocket and the
activity mat, cards, and counters in the right pocket.

MATERIALS

❖ pages 90–99

❖ two-pocket folder

❖ scissors

❖ glue

❖ zipper plastic bag

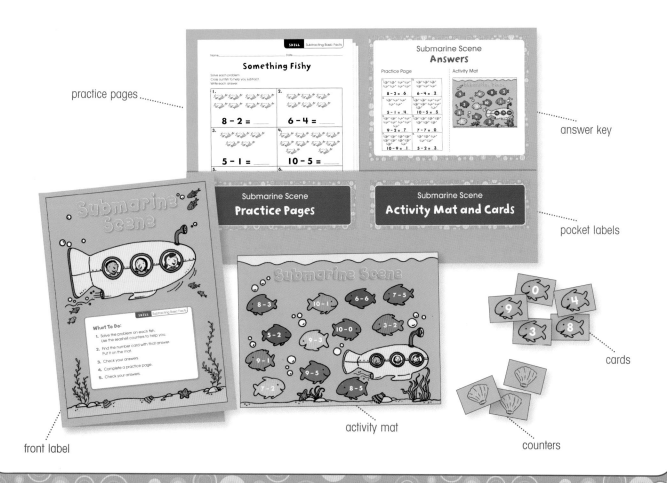

practice pages

answer key

pocket labels

cards

activity mat

counters

front label

Name_____ Date_____

Something Fishy

Solve each problem.
Cross out fish to help you subtract.
Write each answer.

1.

$$8 - 2 = \underline{\hspace{1.5cm}}$$

2.

$$6 - 4 = \underline{\hspace{1.5cm}}$$

3.

$$5 - 1 = \underline{\hspace{1.5cm}}$$

4.

$$10 - 5 = \underline{\hspace{1.5cm}}$$

5.

$$9 - 2 = \underline{\hspace{1.5cm}}$$

6.

$$7 - 7 = \underline{\hspace{1.5cm}}$$

7.

$$10 - 9 = \underline{\hspace{1.5cm}}$$

8.

$$5 - 2 = \underline{\hspace{1.5cm}}$$

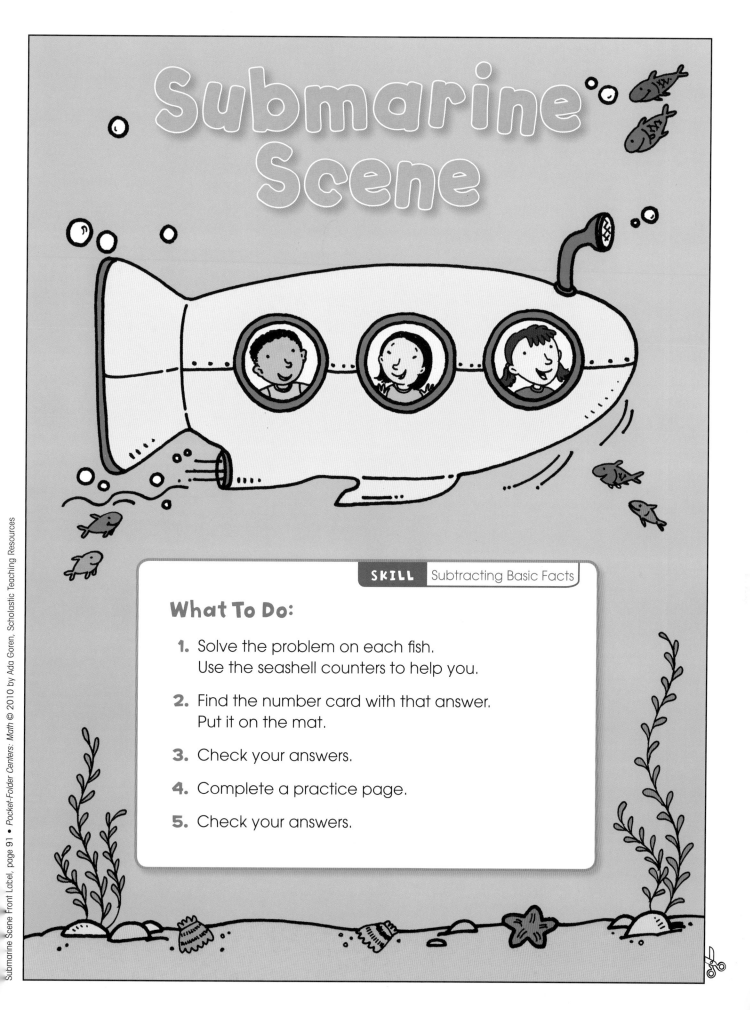

Submarine Scene

SKILL Subtracting Basic Facts

What To Do:

1. Solve the problem on each fish.
   Use the seashell counters to help you.

2. Find the number card with that answer.
   Put it on the mat.

3. Check your answers.

4. Complete a practice page.

5. Check your answers.

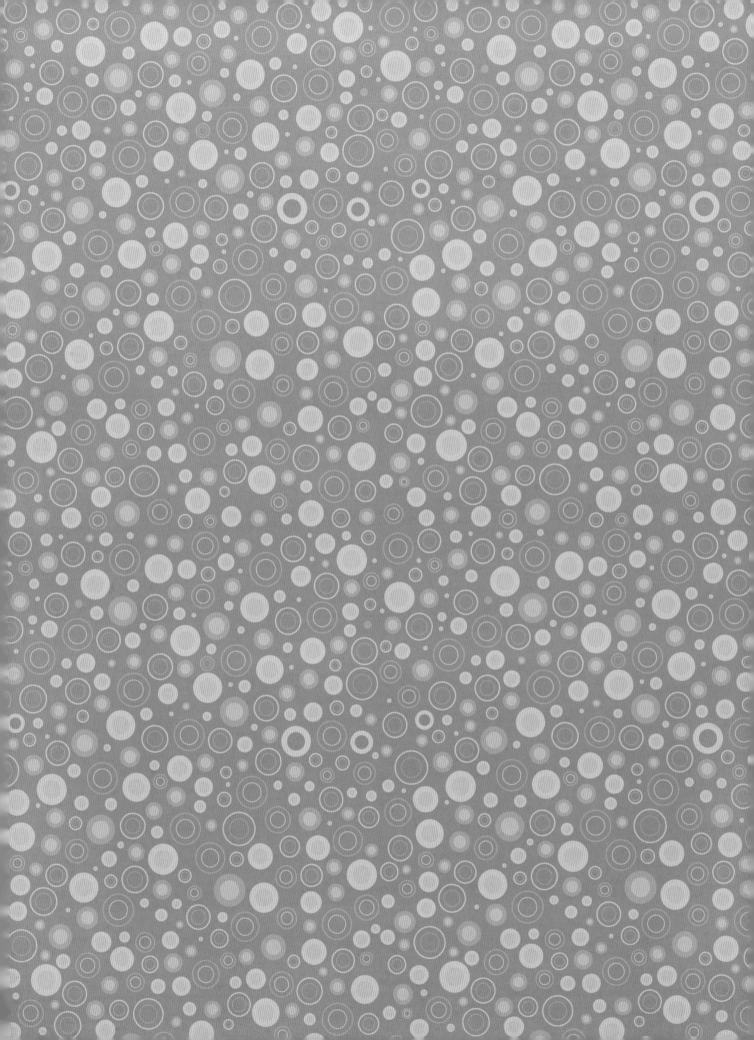

Submarine Scene
Practice Pages

Submarine Scene
Activity Mat and Cards

Submarine Scene
Answers

Practice Page

1. $8 - 2 = \underline{6}$

2. $6 - 4 = \underline{2}$

3. $5 - 1 = \underline{4}$

4. $10 - 5 = \underline{5}$

5. $9 - 2 = \underline{7}$

6. $7 - 7 = \underline{0}$

7. $10 - 9 = \underline{1}$

8. $5 - 2 = \underline{3}$

Activity Mat

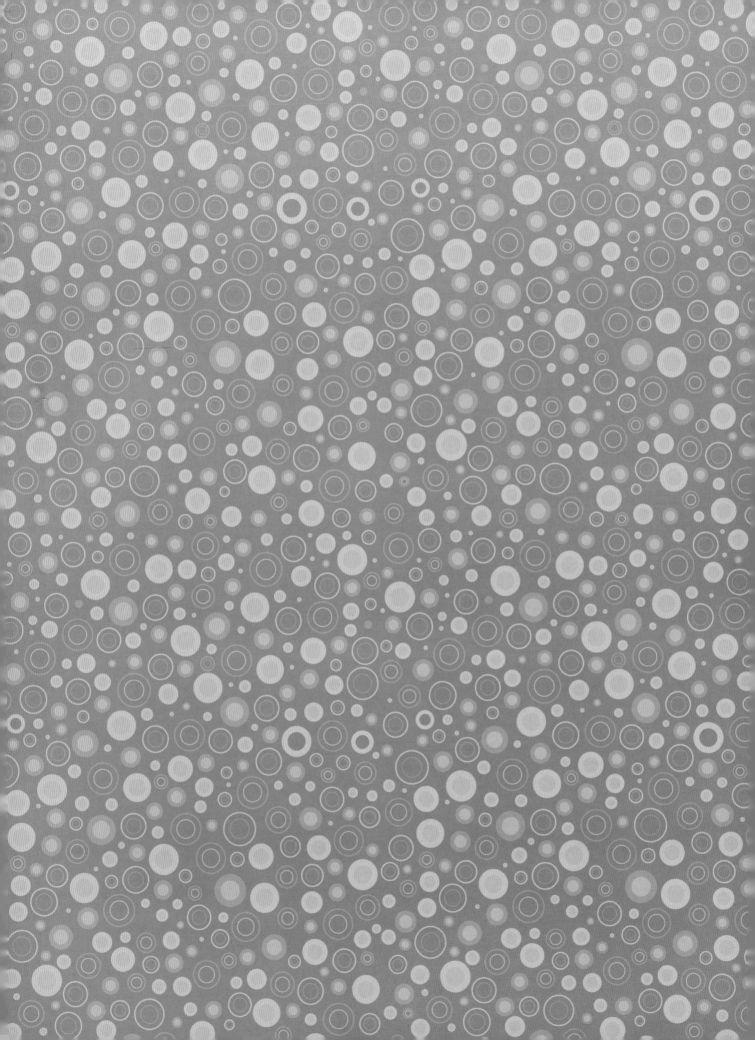

Submarine Scene

$7-5$

$3-2$

$6-6$

$10-0$

$8-5$

$10-1$

$9-3$

$9-5$

$8-3$

$5-2$

$9-1$

$7-2$

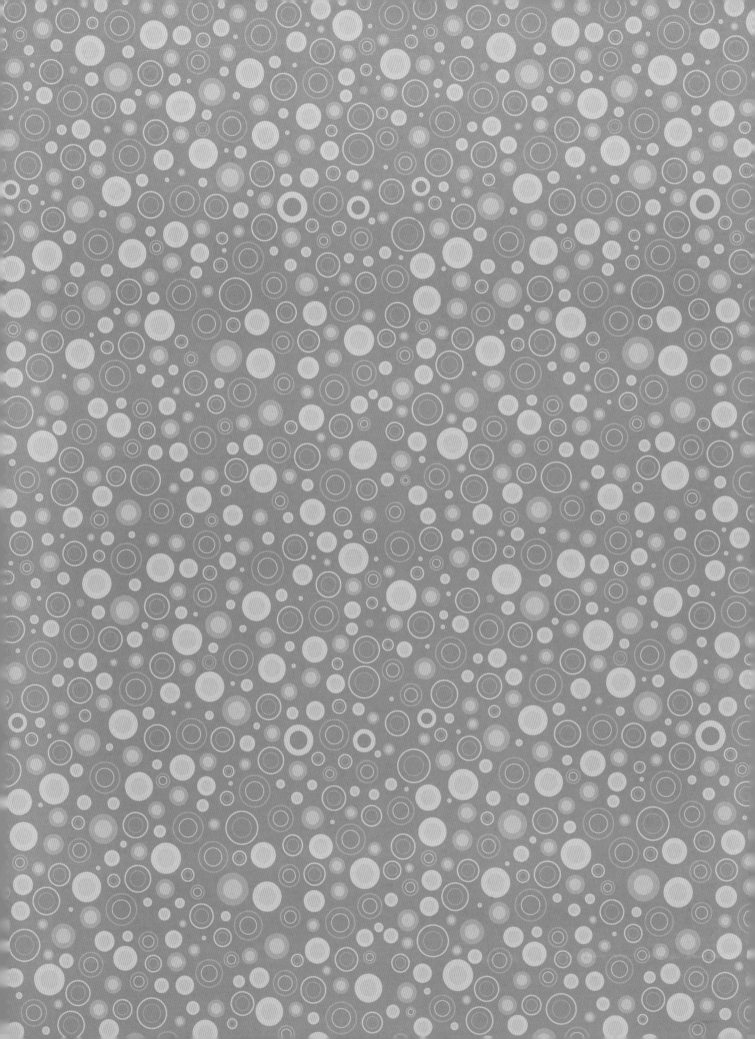

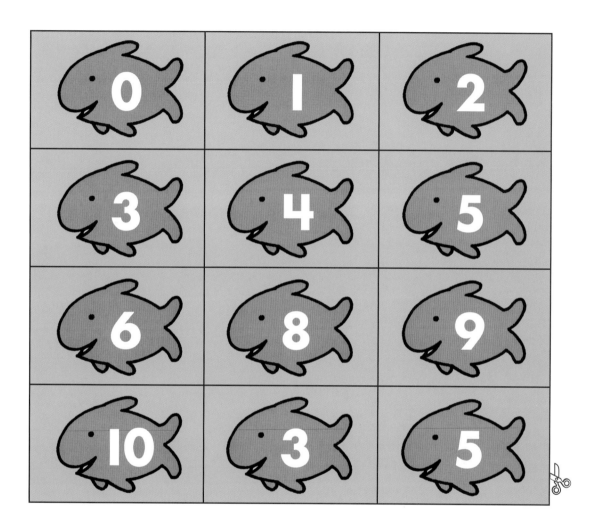

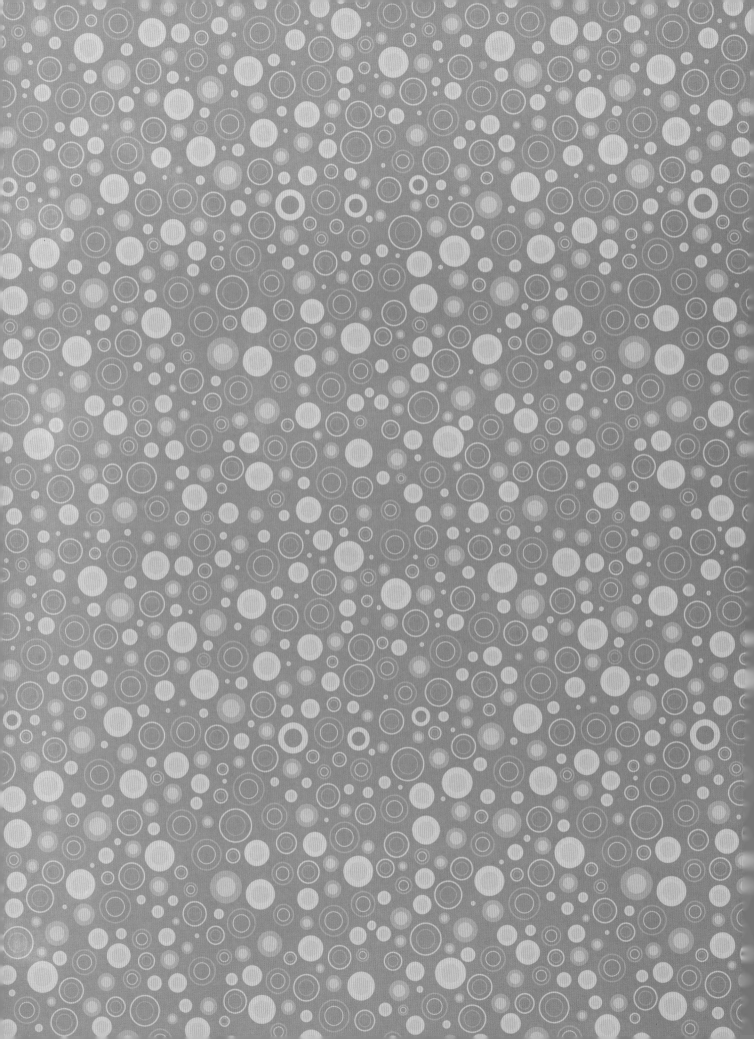

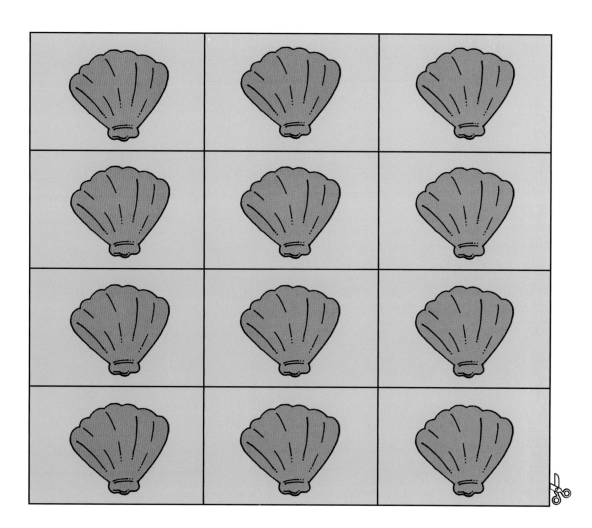

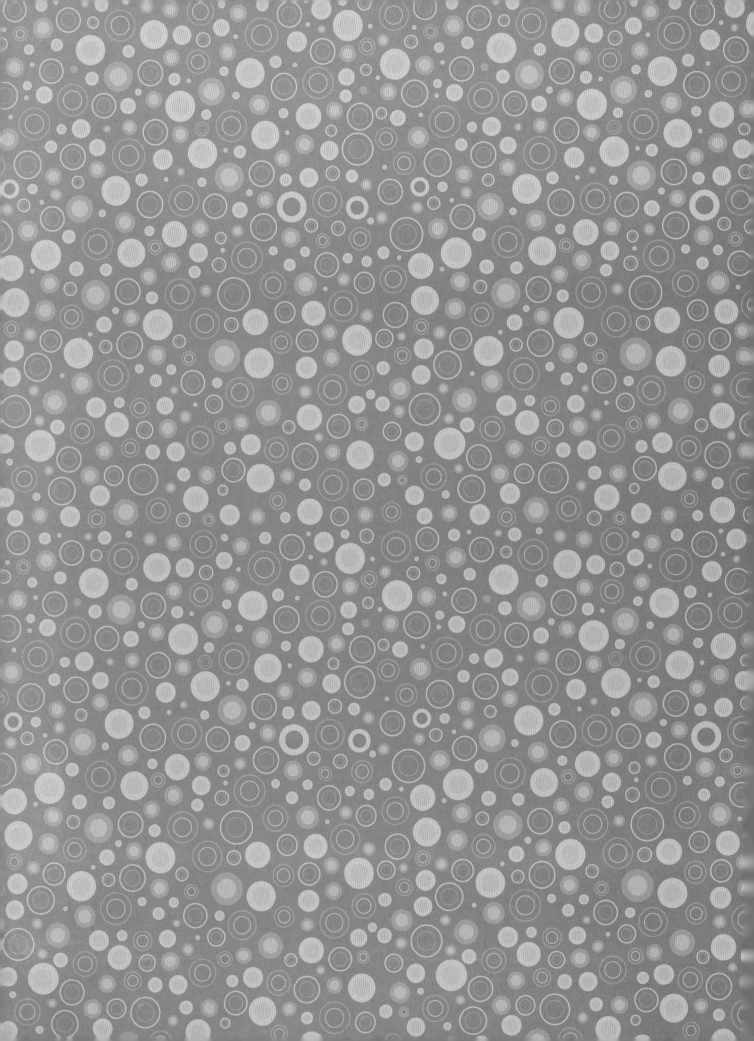

Gems of the Sea

How to Assemble

1. Cut out the front label on page 103. Glue it to the front of the pocket folder.

2. Cut out the pocket labels and answer key on page 105. Glue them to the inside of the folder, as shown.

3. Cut out the activity mat and gem cards on pages 107 and 109. Store the cards in the zipper plastic bag.

4. Make multiple copies of the practice page on page 102.

5. Place the practice pages in the left pocket and the activity mat and cards in the right pocket.

MATERIALS

❖ pages 102–109

❖ two-pocket folder

❖ scissors

❖ glue

❖ zipper plastic bag

practice pages

answer key

pocket labels

front label

activity mat

cards

Name_____ Date_____

Gems of the Sea

Complete the activity mat.
Use the graph to answer the questions.

1. The octopus has _____ rubies.

2. The octopus has _____ emeralds.

3. The octopus has _____ pearls.

4. The octopus has _____ sapphires.

5. The octopus has more of which gem?
   Circle your answer.

          or

6. The octopus has more of which gem?
   Circle your answer.

          or

7. The octopus has the most of which gem?
   Draw your answer.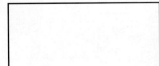

8. The octopus has the fewest of which gem?
   Draw your answer.

Gems of the Sea

SKILL Graphing

What To Do:

1. Fill in the graph.
   Use the gem cards.

2. Check your answers.

3. Complete a practice page.
   Use the graph to find your answers.

4. Check your answers.

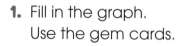

Gems of the Sea
Practice Pages

Gems of the Sea
Activity Mat and Cards

Gems of the Sea
Answers

Practice Page

1. The octopus has **3** rubies.

2. The octopus has **4** emeralds.

3. The octopus has **5** pearls.

4. The octopus has **2** sapphires.

5. The octopus has more of which gem?
   Circle your answer.

   pearl or ruby

6. The octopus has more of which gem?
   Circle your answer.

   emerald or sapphire

7. The octopus has the most of which gem?
   Draw your answer.

8. The octopus has the fewest of which gem?
   Draw your answer.

Activity Mat

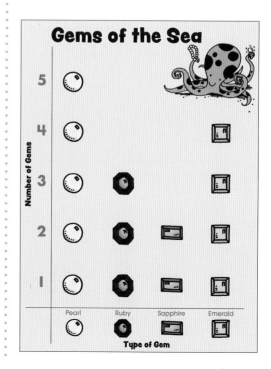

Gems of the Sea

Number of Gems

5

4

3

2

1

Pearl	Ruby	Sapphire	Emerald

Type of Gem

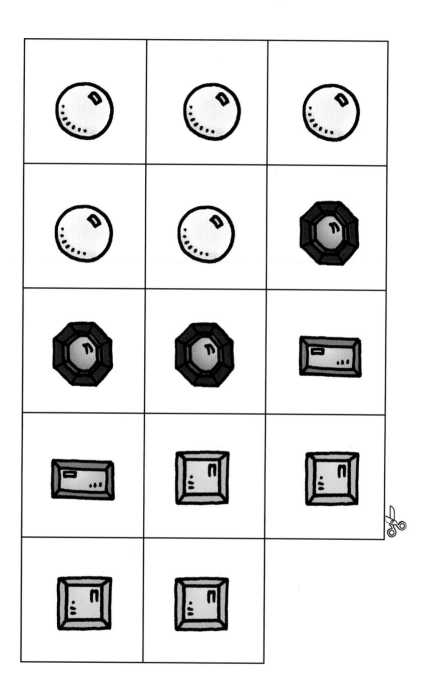

Duck's Diner

How to Assemble

1. Cut out the front label on page 113. Glue it to the front of the pocket folder.

2. Cut out the pocket labels and answer key on page 115. Glue them to the inside of the folder, as shown.

3. Cut out the activity mat and coin cards on pages 117 and 119. Store the cards in the zipper plastic bag.

4. Make multiple copies of the practice page on page 112.

5. Place the practice pages in the left pocket and the activity mat and cards in the right pocket.

MATERIALS

❖ pages 112–119

❖ two-pocket folder

❖ scissors

❖ glue

❖ zipper plastic bag

TIP: Have scissors and glue handy for children to complete the practice page.

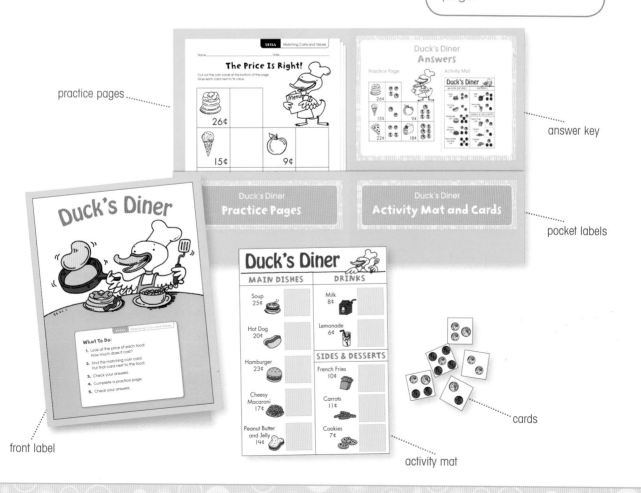

practice pages

answer key

pocket labels

front label

cards

activity mat

Name_____ Date_____

The Price Is Right!

Cut out the coin cards at the bottom of the page.
Glue each card next to its value.

Duck's Diner

SKILL Matching Coins and Values

What To Do:

1. Look at the price of each food. How much does it cost?

2. Find the matching coin card. Put that card next to the food.

3. Check your answers.

4. Complete a practice page.

5. Check your answers.

Duck's Diner
Practice Pages

Duck's Diner
Activity Mat and Cards

Duck's Diner
Answers

Practice Page

Activity Mat

Duck's Diner

MAIN DISHES

Soup
25¢

Hot Dog
20¢

Hamburger
23¢

Cheesy
Macaroni
17¢

Peanut Butter
and Jelly
14¢

DRINKS

Milk
8¢

Lemonade
6¢

SIDES & DESSERTS

French Fries
10¢

Carrots
11¢

Cookies
7¢

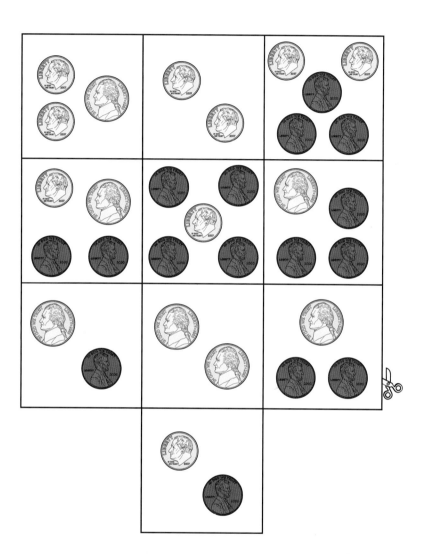

Game Time!

How to Assemble

1. Cut out the front label on page 123. Glue it to the front of the pocket folder.

2. Cut out the pocket labels and answer key on page 125. Glue them to the inside of the folder, as shown.

3. Cut out the activity mat, time cards, and clock hands on pages 127, 129, and 131. Store the cards in the zipper plastic bag.

4. Use the paper brad to attach the clock hands to the clock on the mat.

5. Make multiple copies of the practice page on page 122.

6. Place the practice pages in the left pocket and the activity mat and cards in the right pocket.

MATERIALS

❖ pages 122–131

❖ two-pocket folder

❖ scissors

❖ glue

❖ paper brad

❖ zipper plastic bag

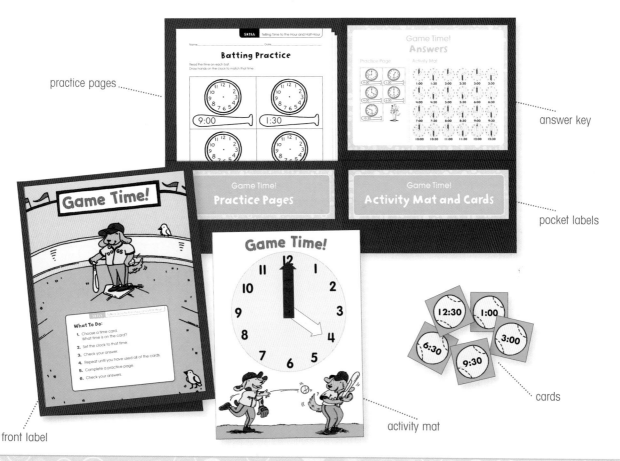

practice pages

answer key

pocket labels

cards

activity mat

front label

Name_____ Date_____

Batting Practice

Read the time on each bat.
Draw hands on the clock to match that time.

Game Time! Practice Page • Pocket-Folder Centers: Math © 2010 by Ada Goren, Scholastic Teaching Resources

Game Time!

SKILL Telling Time to the Hour and Half-Hour

What To Do:

1. Choose a time card.
   What time is on the card?

2. Set the clock to that time.

3. Check your answer.

4. Repeat until you have used all of the cards.

5. Complete a practice page.

6. Check your answers.

Game Time!
Answers

Practice Page

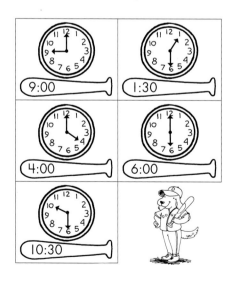

Activity Mat

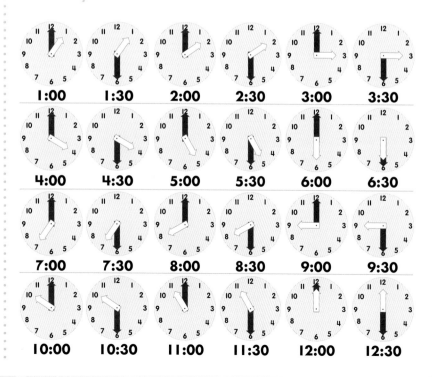

Game Time!

131

Monkey Measures

How to Assemble

1. Cut out the front label on page 135. Glue it to the front of the pocket folder.

2. Cut out the pocket labels and answer key on page 137. Glue them to the inside of the folder, as shown.

3. Cut out the activity mat and banana cards on pages 139, 141, and 143. Store one set of the cards in the zipper plastic bag.

4. Make multiple copies of the practice page on page 134.

5. Place the practice pages in the left pocket and the activity mat and cards in the right pocket.

MATERIALS

❖ pages 134–143

❖ two-pocket folder

❖ scissors

❖ glue

❖ zipper plastic bag

TIPS:

• Have scissors handy for children to complete the practice page.

• Use the extra set of banana cards (page 143) to replace worn or lost cards.

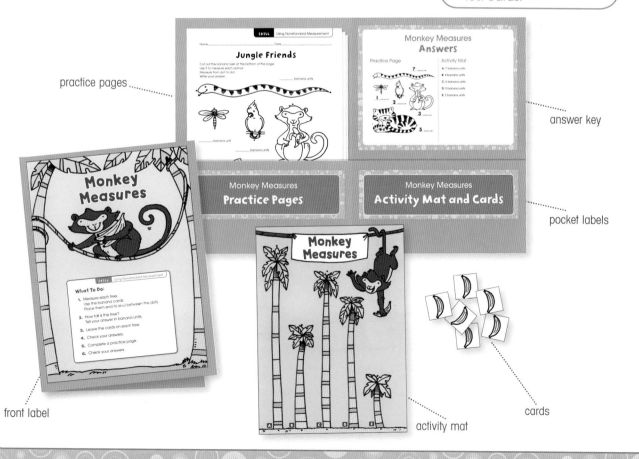

practice pages

answer key

pocket labels

front label

activity mat

cards

Name_____ Date_____

Jungle Friends

Cut out the banana ruler at the bottom of the page.
Use it to measure each animal.
Measure from dot to dot.
Write your answer.

_____ banana units

_____ banana unit

_____ banana units

_____ banana units

_____ banana units

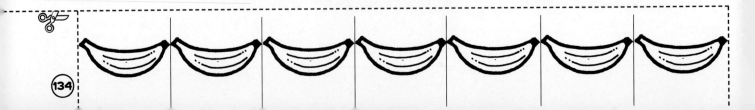

Monkey Measures

SKILL Using Nonstandard Measurement

What To Do:

1. Measure each tree.
Use the banana cards.
Place them end to end between the dots.

2. How tall is the tree?
Tell your answer in banana units.

3. Leave the cards on each tree.

4. Check your answers.

5. Complete a practice page.

6. Check your answers.

Monkey Measures
Practice Pages

Monkey Measures
Activity Mat and Cards

Monkey Measures
Answers

Practice Page

7 banana units

1 banana unit

2 banana units

3 banana units

5 banana units

Activity Mat

A: 7 banana units

B: 4 banana units

C: 6 banana units

D: 5 banana units

E: 2 banana units

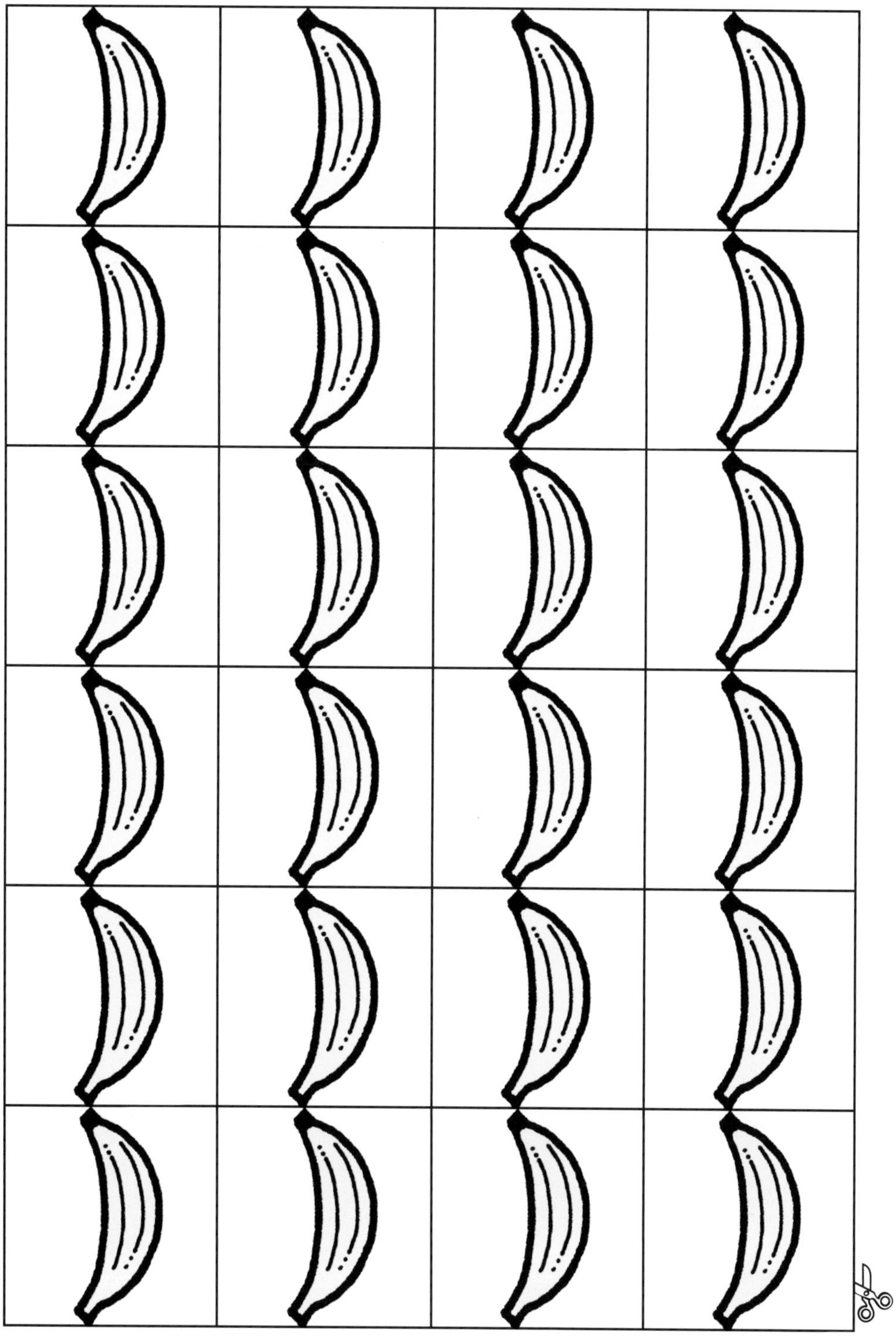

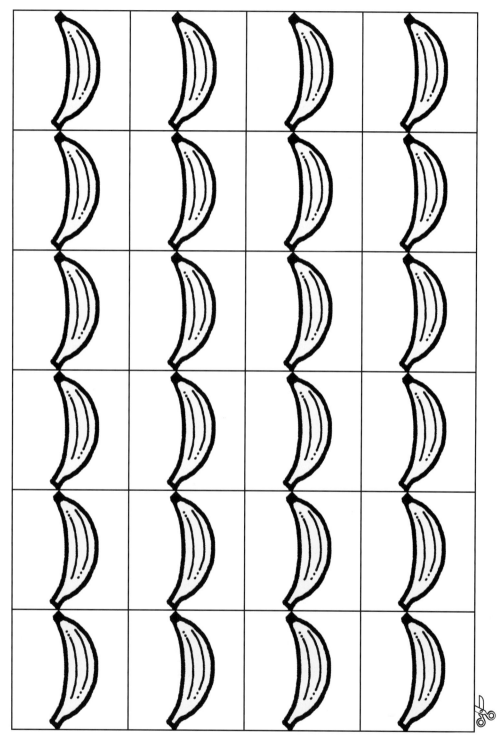

extra cards